Child's Play

Michael McGuire as FATHER MOZIAN, Fritz
Weaver as JEROME MALLEY, Robbie Reed as
BANKS, Pat Hingle as JOSEPH DOBBS, Peter Mac-
Lean as FATHER GRIFFIN and David Rounds as
FATHER PENNY.

Child's Play

by Robert Marasco

Random House

New York

Photographs by courtesy of Martha Swope

Library of Congress Catalog Card Number: 70-125599

Manufactured in the United States of America

FIRST PRINTING

For George Ziegler and Conn Gibney

Phoebus, our lord, plainly orders us
to drive out a defiling thing which, he says,
has been harbored in this land.

—Oedipus Rex

CHILD'S PLAY *was first presented on February 17, 1970, by David Merrick at the Royale Theatre in New York City with the following cast*:

Faculty

PAUL REESE	Ken Howard
FATHER GEORGE PENNY	David Rounds
FATHER WILLIAM GRIFFIN	Peter MacLean
JEROME MALLEY	Fritz Weaver
JOSEPH DOBBS	Pat Hingle
FATHER FRANK MOZIAN	Michael McGuire

Students

CARRE	Bryant Fraser
MEDLEY	Christopher Deane
BANKS	Robbie Reed
JENNINGS	Mark Hall
O'DONNELL	Frank Fiore
SHEA	Patrick Shea
WILSON	Ron Martin
MCARDLE	Lloyd Kramer
TRAVIS	John Handy

Directed by Joseph Hardy
Associate Producer Samuel Liff
Scenery and lighting by Jo Mielziner
Costumes by Sara Brook
Sound created by Gary Harris

THE SCENE

The action takes place at St. Charles' School. The time is the present, a week in midwinter.

Child's Play

The scene is the lay Faculty Room and the adjacent staircase and corridor in St. Charles', a Catholic boarding school for boys. Both areas are vast, Gothic, with huge arches disappearing into the shadows above. Windows in the Faculty Room, framed by dusty red drapes, reach up two stories, cut in half by a balcony which has now become a cluttered office area containing files, a ditto machine, typewriter, etc. Doors lead to this balcony from an upper landing in the hall area, and from the offstage stairway leading down to the Faculty Room.

Directly under the balcony is JEROME MALLEY'S private area, a small alcove with a wing chair, a lamp, and a library table piled with books. Across the room is JOSEPH DOBBS' worn leather chair, a small table with a lamp, a phone and a few textbooks. A common work table, with three chairs, is set in front of a massive Renaissance fireplace. Near the table are a cupboard, a bookcase with a few cups, a hotplate, a coffeepot, a small refrigerator— JOSEPH DOBBS' touches of comfort in the room.

A door at the left leads to a locker room and lavatory, and to the balcony stairs offstage. Another door at the right leads to the hall area.

In the hall, the staircase descends to the floor below. The balustrades are huge, with a statue of a saint atop the

3

center newel. The staircase continues up to the next floor. There is an open area in front of the stairs, and a corridor leading back past the Faculty Room door and off to the right, under the stairs.

It is three o'clock on an afternoon in midwinter. The Faculty Room is dimly lit as the curtain rises. PAUL REESE, *a teacher in his early twenties, genial, athletic-looking, is seated at the work table, reading. The hall lights come up as a class bell rings.* REESE *gets up slowly and goes into the lavatory.*

With the bell, the boys begin to appear from the gym area down the corridor, and at the top of the staircase. FATHER PENNY, *a rather aristocratic-looking young priest, is coming down the stairs, brushing past the boys. He wears a cassock with a sash, as do all the priests of this order. He is carrying a schoolbag and a freshly typed stencil. As he reaches the landing and starts for the Faculty Room, a boy,* JENNINGS, *steps in front of him and blocks his passage. The other boys stop all movement.* FATHER PENNY *makes an attempt to get past* JENNINGS *but can't. There is silence in the corridor.*

FATHER PENNY   Get out of my way.

(FATHER GRIFFIN, *the prefect of discipline, appears at the top of the staircase. The boys continue to stare at* FATHER PENNY *and* JENNINGS)

FATHER GRIFFIN   You heard what he said. Get out of his way.

(*There is a pause.* JENNINGS *steps aside slowly,*

4

allowing FATHER PENNY *to move toward the Faculty Room.* FATHER GRIFFIN *comes down the stairs, clipboard in hand*)

FATHER PENNY (*Going into the Faculty Room*) Bastards!

FATHER GRIFFIN (*Coming down the stairs*) All right, Martin, Callino—move! And you, Jennings, go down and wait outside my office. (*He crosses in front of* JEN-NINGS *and stops when he sees that none of the boys have moved*) You heard what I said. Go downstairs and wait outside my office. (JENNINGS *pauses before taking a step toward* FATHER GRIFFIN, *challenging him. There is a pause, and then* FATHER GRIFFIN *slaps him hard across the face. No one moves.* JENNINGS *stands defiantly, inviting another blow.* FATHER GRIFFIN'S *eyes shift quickly to the other boys, who remain motionless, watching him tensely*) Keep moving! (*No one does.* JEROME MALLEY *begins to descend the stairs, carrying texts and his red markbook. He is in his mid-forties, tall, somewhat forbidding. He wears a dark three-piece suit. He does not look at the boys, who remain quiet but make way for him to pass.* MALLEY *acknowledges* FATHER GRIFFIN *as he passes him on his way to the Faculty Room*)

(JENNINGS *turns slowly now and starts downstairs. Gradually the other boys begin to move*)

FATHER GRIFFIN (*Lamely; more rattled than angry*) All right, lift those feet!

5

(*He looks after them a moment, then down at his
hand. He goes back up the stairs and out, to the
right.*
During all this, FATHER PENNY *has gone up to the
dittoing machine on the balcony. He is running
off a biology test.* MALLEY, *seemingly distracted
and angry, has put his books down on the common
table, and sits down in his study area.*
DOBBS *and a boy,* MCARDLE, *can be heard coming
up the stairs.* DOBBS *is in his late fifties, the oldest
teacher on the faculty. He wears an old corduroy
jacket—rumpled and comfortable, like* DOBBS *himself. They reach the corridor outside the Faculty
Room*)

DOBBS   All right, McArdle, I'll see the headmaster for you.
But you knew that call would upset Mr. Malley. So
why'd you do it?

MCARDLE   It was just a joke, Mr. Dobbs.

DOBBS   The joke is that he recognized your voice. If you
fellows called me in the middle of the night, I'd have
you on the carpet, too.

MCARDLE   Yeah, but you wouldn't have me thrown out
of here.

DOBBS   You haven't been thrown out yet.

MCARDLE   Well, give him time. He's mean enough to do
it. Lash would really get a charge out of that.

DOBBS McArdle, don't call him Lash. (MEDLEY, *a boy in a gym suit, appears behind* DOBBS. *He is carrying a basketball*) He's Mr. Malley to you.

MCARDLE Well, it's the truth, sir. He enjoys watching us sweat it out. I mean, there's gotta be something wrong with a man like that. All the guys say so.

DOBBS I don't care what all the guys say. (MEDLEY *bounces the basketball—loudly, deliberately—to* MC-ARDLEY. DOBBS *turns to face him*) What do you want, Medley?

(MEDLEY *keeps his eyes on* MCARDLE. *There is an obvious silent communication between the two boys*)

MCARDLE Time for basketball practice.

DOBBS (*Looking from one to the other*) I'll tell Mr. Reese; you go on.

MEDLEY (*Without moving*) I need the ball, sir.

(DOBBS *nods at* MCARDLE, *whose hands have tightened around the ball. There is a long pause; the boys continue to stare at each other*)

DOBBS (*Puzzled*) Give him the ball. (MCARDLE *waits,*

then bounces the ball to MEDLEY: *the same loud signal. The boy catches the ball but does not move*) Medley, I thought I told you to go on. (*There is a pause. Then the boy leaves.* DOBBS *turns back to* MCARDLE) What is it with you fellows lately?

MCARDLE (*Quickly*)   I have to go, sir.

DOBBS (*Put off by the change in him*)   What? Yes, all right. I'll see if I can find Mr. Malley . . . (MCARDLE *is moving away*) But remember, no promises.

MCARDLE   Yes, sir. Thank you.

(*The boy leaves;* DOBBS *is watching him*)

DOBBS (*Calling, at the door*)   McArdle . . . ?

(*There is no reply.* MALLEY *hears the boy's name and rises.* DOBBS *stands there a moment, his hand on the doorknob. He gives a puzzled shake of his head as he enters the Faculty Room.* MALLEY *turns away and picks up a book*)

FATHER PENNY (*Greeting*)   Mr. Dobbs.

DOBBS (*Looks up to the balcony*)   Father Penny. Working after the final bell. Admirable.

(*He places his books on the table and turns on the electric percolator*)

FATHER PENNY I have a biology test to run off . . . fodder for filthy little minds. I'll be through with the machine in a moment.

DOBBS I won't be using it, Father. (*Calling* REESE, *who's in the lavatory*) Youngsters want to know if Mr. Reese can come out to play.

REESE Be right out!

(MALLEY *and* DOBBS *do not look at each other.* REESE *comes out of the lavatory. He has changed into a sweat suit. He bustles around the room*)

REESE Where's my whistle?

(*He goes to a cabinet*)

DOBBS (*Takes a whistle out of* REESE's *canvas bag, and hands it to* REESE) How about that?

REESE How'd it get there? (*Puts the whistle around his neck*) Don't suppose I can interest you in a game of kick-the-can?

DOBBS With the wee ones? Father Penny's your man.

FATHER PENNY (*Acknowledging the reference as he turns the mimeo machine*) . . . fifty-three . . .

REESE How 'bout showing the fellows what a regular guy you are, hunh, Father?

(*He heads for the lavatory, looking for his keys*)

FATHER PENNY Thanks, but my truss is being laundered.

REESE (*Laughs*) You're a flabby bunch.

DOBBS (*Busy at the work table; refers to* REESE) I taught this one when he was a freshman here, Father; wonderful, how some people never seem to change . . . What are you looking for now?

REESE Keys, keys.

(DOBBS *reaches for a ring of keys under* REESE's *books on the table and throws them to* REESE)

DOBBS How about that? I suppose that's why he gets on so well with the boys; emotionally he's just about a year behind them.

(*He sits looking through his schoolbag*)

REESE Mr. Chips, what did you teach me, anyway?

DOBBS   Obviously nothing.

REESE   That cuts both ways, doesn't it?

(MALLEY *goes into the locker-room area, offstage*)

DOBBS   I was the first layman they hired, the old Fathers. (*Pointing to* REESE) Look what it's led to.

REESE   Charm, vitality.

FATHER PENNY (*Sarcastically*) . . . sixty-seven . . .

(FATHER GRIFFIN *reappears at the head of the stairs and starts down*)

REESE   I gotta go.

DOBBS   Please do. (*To* FATHER PENNY *as he goes toward the kitchenette*) Cup of coffee, Father?

FATHER PENNY   No, devil's brew.

REESE (*At the door*)   Be here later?

DOBBS   I've been here thirty years. I'll be here later.

(REESE *starts to go toward the gym.* FATHER GRIF-FIN *sees* REESE *and calls to him*)

FATHER GRIFFIN Paul!

REESE (*Turning to him*) Hello, Father.

FATHER GRIFFIN Going to the gym?

REESE Yeah. How 'bout a game of handball?

FATHER GRIFFIN I'll take a rain check on that.

(MALLEY *comes out of the locker room*)

REESE (*Starts for the gym*) Whenever you say.

FATHER GRIFFIN Listen, Paul, do me a favor— (REESE *moves over to* FATHER GRIFFIN) Keep an eye on the kids.

REESE Sure, what's wrong?

FATHER GRIFFIN Just watch them. If they get out of hand, clear the gym.

REESE Anybody in particular?

FATHER GRIFFIN Yes, all of them. I'll be in here or down in my office if you want me.

(*He starts to go downstairs*)

REESE   Okay. That it?

FATHER GRIFFIN   That's it.

REESE   Tomorrow on that handball game, hunh?

FATHER GRIFFIN   Let you know tomorrow. (REESE *goes out toward the gym.* FATHER GRIFFIN *calls after him*) Paul! Watch them.

REESE (*Offstage*)   Sure, sure.

(FATHER GRIFFIN *looks down the corridor, and moves toward the rear, out of view briefly.* FATHER PENNY *is still at the machine*)

FATHER PENNY (*Triumphant*)   One hundred!

DOBBS   A shaft for the boys, is it?

(*He pours a cup of coffee*)

FATHER PENNY   Something to drive them back into the woodwork.

DOBBS   Ah, yes, it's that time of year—the long push toward Easter.

FATHER PENNY (*Arranging test papers*)   It's always that time of year.

DOBBS   These are the dark months; or the hornbusters . . . depending on which side of the desk you sit.

FATHER PENNY   We'll see whose horns go first—theirs or mine.

FATHER GRIFFIN   (*Comes back to the door and enters the room. Looking up at* FATHER PENNY) Bellyachin' as usual, George?

(DOBBS *pours another cup of coffee*)

FATHER PENNY   The goon squad . . . The pain, alas, is not in the belly, but rather *ad podicem.* In the ass to you.

FATHER GRIFFIN   (*Closing the door*) George, you are very erudite. (MALLEY *has once more absorbed himself in a book*) How are you, Joe?

(*He puts his clipboard on the table; sits in a chair and lights a cigarette*)

DOBBS   My, my—more clergy in the secular compound. Does this mean an Inquisition? Cup of coffee, Father?

FATHER GRIFFIN   Yes, thanks, Joe. (*He takes the coffee*) George, you didn't mean to send fifteen kids to detention today, did you?

FATHER PENNY   (*Putting papers into his bag*) Have they all been proscribed?

FATHER GRIFFIN They're all here.

FATHER PENNY Then fifteen it was. Every one of them a killer at heart.

FATHER GRIFFIN Sending a kid to detention is serious, George.

FATHER PENNY Thanks for the advice. Read through the list. I think you'll find the evidence warrants it.

(FATHER GRIFFIN *gets up and walks to the fireplace.* MALLEY *moves down to the table to pick up his red markbook, then heads for the door.* DOBBS *calls after him*)

DOBBS Jerome . . . (MALLEY *stops at the door as* DOBBS *starts to move toward him*) Can I speak to you for a minute?

MALLEY The headmaster is waiting.

(*He moves out into the corridor;* DOBBS *follows*)

DOBBS Yes, I know . . . (*Following* MALLEY) Excuse me, Father . . . (*Catching* MALLEY *just before he starts downstairs*) . . . it's about McArdle.

MALLEY Yes?

DOBBS   Jerome, it's . . . not my place, I know, but if you could manage to go a little easy on the boy . . .

MALLEY   You're right, Dobbs, it's not your place. You were speaking to him just now. Why?

DOBBS   The boy is frightened. Jerome, it was an innocent phone call, an adolescent prank. Why crucify him for that?

MALLEY   You'd let it pass, wouldn't you?

DOBBS   I've let worse than that pass. McArdle's a good boy; a little imprudent maybe, but certainly there was no malice intended.

MALLEY   Your solicitude is very touching, Dobbs; it always is. This does *not* concern you.

DOBBS   But it does; the boy will be graduating in June.

MALLEY   (*Starts down the stairs*)   I'm late.

DOBBS   Don't ask the headmaster to expel him, not for an innocent prank.

MALLEY   And if I didn't . . . wouldn't that disappoint you?

DOBBS   Jerome! As a favor . . .

MALLEY   To you?

DOBBS   To the boy.

MALLEY   Don't be ridiculous.

> (*He goes down the stairs.* DOBBS *looks after him,
> then returns to the room.* FATHER PENNY *has come
> down from the balcony. He pulls a paper from his
> bag and begins to speak as* DOBBS *comes back in*)

FATHER PENNY   Would you like to see exhibit A? The
Travis boy. (*Reads paper*) "The male reproductive cells
are formed in the organs known as the balls." (DOBBS
is amused) Condoning it, Mr. Dobbs? *Blasphemy*,
considering my office, my charisma? What has happened
to the Judeo-Christian tradition?

FATHER GRIFFIN   George generally sleeps in the reliquary,
just behind the main altar.

FATHER PENNY (*Snapping shut his bag*)   Father Griffin,
you can see, has been a great comfort to me during my
trial in this wilderness. Seven priests and three laymen
on the faculty; why am *I* always the victim?

FATHER GRIFFIN   Has it all been that bad, George?

FATHER PENNY Every day I mount the pillory of that podium, exposing myself to those monsters who sit there dissecting me as if I were some large anointed frog. Do you know what they call me? Do you have any idea?

DOBBS It's never flattering if it's any good.

FATHER PENNY King Kong. *King Kong.*

FATHER GRIFFIN Could've been a helluva lot worse, eh, Joe?

FATHER PENNY Quiet, you! One day I happened to ask them, "But who is this Kong individual you keep referring to? A new boy come from the East? A pious devotion?" Jeers and catcalls, of course. I gave them a test immediately.

(*He moves to the door*)

DOBBS You have my sympathy, Father. There's nothing more deflating than fifteen minutes on a platform in front of those keen young eyes.

FATHER PENNY Ah, they're gifted with a higher vision, then? Those unwashed hordes whooping up and down the stairwells? Horse shit!

(*He opens the door*)

FATHER GRIFFIN Where're you going, George?

FATHER PENNY Into shock.

(He slams the door as he goes downstairs)

FATHER GRIFFIN *(Calls)* Watch the dark stretches, George!

DOBBS I never know quite how to take him.

FATHER GRIFFIN George is all right. *(Trying to order his thoughts, he pauses, then looks at* DOBBS*)* What's wrong with them, Joe?

DOBBS *(Trying to follow)* Wrong?

FATHER GRIFFIN The kids . . . what *is* it with them?

DOBBS They're always jumpy after midterms. It's their way of unwinding.

FATHER GRIFFIN That's what it's called, hunh? *(Picks up his clipboard and goes over to* DOBBS*)* You ever see eighty kids on a detention list before? You managed to nail a few yourself?

DOBBS I'm getting old and crochety.

FATHER GRIFFIN Joe . . . something is wrong with them.

Have you been watching them? Between classes, on the stairs, in the gym after school?

DOBBS   The gym I leave to young Mr. Reese.

FATHER GRIFFIN   Well, watch them sometime. We've never had so many kids getting hurt around here. Hell, if it were just good old vandalism, protest; but they're going *at* one another. Deliberately, whenever they can, they try to hurt one another . . . physical hurt.

DOBBS   Father, I don't believe that.

FATHER GRIFFIN   Believe it! And then try to get something out of them. (*Moves around the table to* DOBBS' *chair*)   You ask how'd it happen and the kid'll just look up at you and shrug. Yesterday a brawl in the dormitory and a kid breaks an arm; the day before, that accident in the chem lab. We need your help, Joe . . .

DOBBS   If it's as you say, of course. In thirty years here, though, I've never known a situation that collar couldn't control.

FATHER GRIFFIN   Well, we're getting less starch in them nowadays. (*Puts down his coffee cup*)   You know, it used to scare the hell out of them being sent to detention. They'd be more scared of coming into my office than the headmaster's. Now they seem to go out of their way to get sent down. Some of them—I think they're waiting for me to lay into them.

DOBBS   What do you want me to do, Father?

FATHER GRIFFIN   Speak to Paul and Jerome when you get a chance; and keep your eyes open to see what's going on with the boys.

DOBBS   I'll speak to young Reese, but Jerome isn't going to pay much attention to anything I have to say.

FATHER GRIFFIN   Think it would be better coming from me?

DOBBS   You or the headmaster. What another teacher does in a classroom is none of my business, I know, but sometimes . . . we can push them too hard.

FATHER GRIFFIN   Jerome's always been rough on the boys, but he's a damn good teacher.

DOBBS   That may be so, but from what the boys are telling me, he's even rougher on them now. They can take so much pressure and who can say how they'll let it out? There was a boy a few years ago, Walter Paxton . . .

FATHER GRIFFIN   Yes, I know about Paxton, but from what I hear it wasn't all Jerome's fault.

DOBBS   Well, maybe not, Father, but I do know the boy couldn't measure up to Jerome's standards. The pressure was too much for him. So one afternoon he went downstairs and tried to hang himself from the pipes in the furnace room. Just like that. Fortunately your predecessor was patrolling the halls at the time.

FATHER GRIFFIN (*A pause*) All right, Joe, I'll speak to Jerome.

DOBBS (*Rising and going to the percolator*) Thank you, Father. Now how about another cup of coffee?

FATHER GRIFFIN No thanks. Time for *me* to start patrolling the halls. (*He starts for the door as* REESE *comes into the room from the gym*) What's wrong?

REESE Nothing. Thirsty . . . need some fuel.

FATHER GRIFFIN Who's with the kids?

REESE One of the seniors. Weyland.

FATHER GRIFFIN One of the seniors is a kid! Paul, you hurry back there.

REESE Okay if I treat the kids?

(*He goes to the refrigerator for a Coke*)

FATHER GRIFFIN Yes, yes. Just don't let them leave the

empties around. (*To* DOBBS) Any other ideas, Joe . . .
please pass them on.

DOBBS   I'll think about it. And let's see more of you here.

(*He goes into the lavatory to rinse the cups*)

FATHER GRIFFIN   Shake a leg, Paul.

(*He leaves and goes downstairs*)

REESE   What're you going to think about?

DOBBS (*Returns from the lavatory; dries and hangs up the
cups*)   Problems. He's worried about the boys.

REESE   What's wrong?

DOBBS   I don't know. Neither does he. You haven't been
having any trouble with them?

REESE (*Taking Cokes from the refrigerator*)   I never have
trouble with anybody.

DOBBS (*Indicating* REESE'*s Coke*)   Real drinks are on me
tonight; a feed too, if I remain *ambulatory*.

REESE   Thanks, but I can't tonight.

DOBBS   Oh? Something on?

REESE   Date.

DOBBS   New girl?

REESE   No, my age.

(*He chuckles*)

DOBBS   She's sharpened your wit, I see. Payday's two days off. What's a witty boy like you using for money?

(REESE *gets up, putting his Coke on the table, then reaches into his canvas bag and pulls out a bag of change. He moves toward* DOBBS)

REESE   It's all right this time. You don't have to bail me out. I finally busted up my piggy bank.

DOBBS (*Peering in*)   By George, must be a dollar in there.

REESE (*Replaces change. He notices* MALLEY'*s schoolbag*) What's Lash doing in here this late? Flogging a kid?

DOBBS (*Pointedly*)   I expect Mr. Malley has a very good reason for being here. Let me remind you, you're one of us now.

REESE (*Gathering Cokes*) I'm sorry. I forget.

DOBBS Well, don't forget.

REESE Hey, Joe, you want to hear something funny? He still scares me, Lash. He scares the hell out of me. I keep expecting him to send me to detention. You know, whenever we have a free period together, I go sit in the john for forty minutes.

DOBBS You're not serious?

REESE So help me! Pretty stupid, hunh?

DOBBS It sure is.

REESE Poor kids, I really feel for them. That lousy red markbook of his could stop a heart. What's he doing working with kids, anyway?

DOBBS I imagine you learned some Latin with Mr. Malley.

REESE Oh, I learned Latin. But I learned English, too, and it wasn't nearly so painful.

DOBBS Well, that's because I'm the grand old man of the faculty, beloved of all the boys.

REESE You're what made me become a teacher. I figured
. . . nice, cushy job; don't have to know much. In fact,
don't really have to know anything. Hell, nobody teaches
English 1 for thirty years.

DOBBS (*Silence; then a look*) It's my vocation, boy. And
it's your vocation, too, let me remind you. Now, don't
you think you'd better get back to the gym, where you're
supposed to be?

(MALLEY *comes into the room, his red markbook in
hand.* REESE *becomes suddenly uneasy*)

REESE (*Quick smile*) Mr. Malley.

MALLEY Reese.

(*He goes to sit in his chair at the table and starts
arranging papers.* REESE *watches self-consciously
as* DOBBS *returns to correcting papers*)

REESE (*Fumbling*) You're . . . around late today.

MALLEY (*Looking up*) Pardon?

REESE You're usually . . . this is late for you.

MALLEY Yes, I suppose it is.

(Gets up to pick up some test papers)

REESE (*Looking at* DOBBS, *who smiles slightly, then back to* MALLEY. *Struggling as he moves toward* MALLEY) I can never get out of here before five. I . . . get involved with the kids and . . . basketball.

MALLEY (*Turning to him; polite, no warmth*) You're enjoying the year?

REESE   Oh, yeah. Yes. The kids are great.

MALLEY   You're not too much older than them yourself, are you?

REESE (*Lamely*)   I guess not.

(*There is a silence.* DOBBS *is obviously listening to* REESE's *discomfort. There is noise from the gym: a distant cheer*)

DOBBS (*Rescuing* REESE)   Isn't that the sound of the rafters being pulled down?

REESE   Hunh?

DOBBS   Your charges are kicking up their heels some.

REESE   Oh, jeez, the kids! (*Grabbing the remaining*

Cokes; to MALLEY) Nice talking to you. Excuse me.

(He exits to the gym. MALLEY *goes to the cabinet where he sharpens his pencil, then returns to sit at the table. Pause)*

DOBBS   All right, Jerome, what about McArdle?

MALLEY *(Busy with papers)* He's been suspended.

DOBBS   How long will he be out?

MALLEY   Indefinitely.

DOBBS   That's a bit harsh, isn't it?

MALLEY   For an innocent prank?

DOBBS   For a senior to miss all that work?

MALLEY   I'm sorry you weren't consulted first. One of your boys, isn't he, Dobbs?

DOBBS   So are they all, Jerome, so are they all. I take it the suspension was the headmaster's idea. You would have preferred expulsion, I'm sure.

MALLEY   Why not ask him yourself? As I understand it,

you'll be going down to see him as soon as I've left the building.

DOBBS The headmaster? Why should I see him?

MALLEY The boy's given him to understand you'll be going down to plead for him.

DOBBS I made no promises.

MALLEY No, you never do. You were misinterpreted as usual.

DOBBS (*Clearing the table of the creamer and sugar bowl*) You've made it quite clear this doesn't concern me.

MALLEY When has that ever stopped you?

DOBBS That's not fair.

MALLEY I'm never fair, Dobbs; your boys must have told you that.

(*More noise is heard from the gym*)

DOBBS Jerome, we spend so much time in this room . . .

(*He slams the refrigerator door and returns to the table*)

MALLEY   I'm trying to work, Dobbs!

DOBBS   I'm sorry I spoke to the boy. It was a mistake.

MALLEY   You deliberately set them against me, the boys. You always have.

DOBBS   That's all in your mind.

(He gets a dust rag from the cupboard and comes back to dust off the table)

MALLEY   It's not in my mind! (Looking directly at DOBBS) You have got to stop undermining my position here.

(Another distant cheer is heard from the gym)

DOBBS   You still don't see it, after all these years. It's not me setting them against you; it's yourself . . . Jerome, the boys are afraid of you. You terrify them. It's as simple as that.

MALLEY   Simpler, Dobbs. You encourage it. Whatever their absurd fears are, you magnify them.

DOBBS   Do I? And what about the counselors and the headmaster, do they encourage it as well? (Going to the cupboard to return the dust rag) Young Reese is uncomfortable being in the same room with you.

MALLEY   Ah yes, you've got yourself an ally there.

DOBBS (*Checks the time of the clock on the mantel; then moves minute hand*)   No one is allied with me against you.

MALLEY   Another in your long line of McArdles.

DOBBS   I'd rather the McArdles than the Paxtons, Jerome. It's a hell of a lot easier on the conscience. (MALLEY *stops; looks up*)   It's the truth isn't it? The boy tried to kill himself. He couldn't take the pressure.

MALLEY   The boy should not have been in this school in the first place. The *work* was too much for him.

DOBBS   Maybe so, but as long as he was here he was our responsibility. (*A long shout from the gym*)   He managed to survive his other classes all right.

MALLEY   Your class.

DOBBS   My class, yes.

MALLEY   What sort of criterion is that?

DOBBS   None, I suppose. Your command of Greek and Latin may be awesome, Jerome, but you know absolutely nothing about boys. Look, all I'm asking is that you ease up on McArdle. Forget methods, forget personalities. For God's sake, what malice can there be in a child?

MALLEY   Listen to me, Dobbs. I'll suffer, since I must, the humiliation of this room with you, and the daily spectacle of a pathetic old man—

DOBBS   All right, Jerome, that's enough.

MALLEY   —living on the affection of adolescent boys—

DOBBS   That's enough, I said!

MALLEY   . . . that *too*, Dobbs, as degrading as it is. But I won't be lectured by you on my responsibility. You are not to see the headmaster! You are not to interfere!

(*Now a cry is heard from the gym, rising to a shriek.* MALLEY *listens without moving.* DOBBS *rushes out into the corridor.* REESE *is coming from the gym area, dragging a boy whose face and gym shirt are covered with blood*)

REESE (*Yelling into the stairwell*)   Father Griffin! Father Griffin! (DOBBS *joins in the cry.* REESE *has gotten the boy to the Faculty Room. He pulls him across the room. The boy,* BANKS, *is screaming, fighting him.* DOBBS *follows*) Oh, God, oh, God, Joe—help me! HELP ME!

(The boy screams louder as DOBBS *and* REESE *bring him into the lavatory.* MALLEY *still does not move. After a pause he turns slightly toward the lavatory as the lights fade)*

FATHER MOZIAN, *the headmaster, a rather commanding figure, is coming up the stairs as the lights build.* MALLEY *has moved into his study area.* FATHER MOZIAN *enters.*

MALLEY   How is the boy, Father?

FATHER MOZIAN   I haven't heard anything yet. Paul's still here, isn't he? (*The phone rings before* MALLEY *can reply.* FATHER MOZIAN *places the leather folder he has been carrying down on* DOBBS' *chair and answers the phone*) Yes, yes, put her through . . . Yes, Mrs. Banks . . . I don't know. Mr. Dobbs is at the hospital with him now. All I know is that there was an accident . . . No, I'm not excusing it, Mrs. Banks. I'm as upset as you are. (DOBBS, *wearing an overcoat, and* FATHER GRIFFIN *come up the stairs and enter the Faculty Room.* FATHER MOZIAN *nods and indicates his impatience with the phone conversation. There is a first-aid kit on the common table.* DOBBS *moves toward it now, and places it back on the shelf*) There's always a teacher in the gym with them.

(REESE *enters from the lavatory, dressed now, but without his jacket*)

34

Ron Martin as WILSON, Frank Fiore as O'DONNELL, Patrick Shea as SHEA, David Rounds as FATHER PENNY, Mark Hall as JENNINGS and John Handy as TRAVIS.

REESE (*To* DOBBS) Christ, this is all my fault!

DOBBS Relax, now relax, will you?

FATHER MOZIAN That has to be your decision, of course, but I don't think it's wise at all . . .

(FATHER GRIFFIN *moves down to* FATHER MOZIAN *with his clipboard*)

FATHER GRIFFIN Eleven boys, Frank.

FATHER MOZIAN (*Anxious to get off the phone*) . . . Look, Mrs. Banks, I'm with the teacher now. (*Looking quickly at* FATHER GRIFFIN's *clipboard*) Can I call you back as soon as I've found out what's happened?

FATHER GRIFFIN (*Moving to* REESE *and showing him the list*) Paul, are these all the boys?

(REESE *looks over the list and nods*)

FATHER MOZIAN Mrs. Banks, he's getting the best of care. That's all I can tell you right now . . . Of course, of course, whenever you say. (*Hangs up. Picks up his folder*) She wants to take him out of the echool. How is Freddy?

DOBBS He's a brave boy but I'm afraid he's going to lose an eye.

(REESE *is putting on his jacket at the cabinet. He stops*)

FATHER MOZIAN   Dear God!

REESE (*In disbelief*)   Lose his eye . . . ?

FATHER MOZIAN (*Moves to the table and sits down, trying to control himself*)   You know what she said to me? "What are you doing to those boys?" Not just *my* boy, *those* boys. (*Angrily*) What happened down there, Paul?

REESE   I don't know! I was there, I saw it all happen and I swear I don't understand it.

FATHER GRIFFIN   They just went for him, is that it?

REESE   No, they were tossing the ball around, playing . . .

DOBBS   Dodge-ball, I've seen them playing it.

FATHER MOZIAN   That can get pretty rough, can't it?

REESE   Not the way they were playing—just killing time till they got enough men together for a game. They were lined up, three or four on either side of the gym.

FATHER GRIFFIN Then you really weren't paying much attention to the game.

REESE I was. I remembered what you said. I was sitting on the benches, waiting to ref the game, talking to some of the seniors.

FATHER GRIFFIN Well, you were in here getting Cokes. How long did you stay?

DOBBS (*To* FATHER GRIFFIN) Not long, Father, no more than five minutes.

(MALLEY *remains in the alcove, listening almost guiltily. He has gotten his coat from the closet; he places it on the back of his chair, careful not to distract anyone in the center of the room. During the next exchange, he gathers the rest of his books quickly, becoming more absorbed in* REESE'S *narration. Gradually he stops and listens*)

FATHER MOZIAN (*Sitting in* MALLEY'S *chair at the table*) Go on, Paul.

REESE (*Moving nervously*) Well, Holleran got the ball and flipped it to McCarthy and McCarthy flipped it to the kid next to him. Then they sort of . . . formed a circle, very slowly.

(*He illustrates with his hands*)

FATHER MOZIAN   As if it were something planned?

DOBBS   (*Explaining it away*)   Of course it's planned. What game doesn't have rules?

REESE   Let me finish. The fellows kept flipping the ball to one another. They didn't stop flipping it while they were changing position . . . just flipping the ball. So I said, "What's up, guys?" But they didn't seem to hear me . . . just flipping the ball to one another—real serious, their faces, and silence—flipping the ball and forming this circle.

FATHER GRIFFIN   And you were still up on the benches.

(MALLEY *is changing his shoes, putting on rubbers*)

REESE   No! I was down on the court with them.

FATHER GRIFFIN   Then why didn't you break it up?

REESE   Why should I? All they were doing was flipping the ball back and forth.

FATHER MOZIAN   It's possible that you missed some kind of signal, isn't it?

REESE   No, I don't think so. Freddy had the ball and held it for maybe a couple of seconds longer than the other guys . . . and they were all looking at him, not saying anything, just looking.

DOBBS   Of course they were looking at him, the boy had the ball.

REESE (*Crossing to* DOBBS)   No, no. Joe, this was different. They were staring at him. And so I said, "Okay, Freddy, let's go!" But they didn't seem to hear me, they were all staring at Freddy . . . blank, no expression.

FATHER MOZIAN   Isn't that when you should have stopped them?

REESE (*His voice rising*)   All right, I should have. I didn't! (*Stops himself*) . . . Freddy waited, maybe for a few seconds, then he flipped the ball and walked into the middle of the circle . . . and they all waited until he was in the center. I could see him take a deep breath and I said, (*Looks to* FATHER GRIFFIN) "Okay, let's break it up, you guys!" And just as I said it, I saw the guy with the ball step back a few feet . . . (*Looks to* DOBBS) and Freddy was watching him . . . (*Looks back to* FATHER MOZIAN) and this guy lifted the ball over his shoulder. And then, then he let go and smashed it into Freddy's stomach. I could see Freddy's arms come in—like this—and then . . . God! They—stopped —just before the ball hit him.

(*He illustrates the reflex*)

FATHER MOZIAN   He didn't try to protect himself?

DOBBS   Of course he did.

REESE   I swear he didn't!

DOBBS   Someone throws something at you, you—

REESE   (*Very worked up now*)   His arms stopped—here!
I heard the ball hit him, and he doubled over . . . And
when it hit him, the kids—the kids . . . let out a cry—
not a cry, a kind of . . . cheer! A cheer! I heard it.

FATHER GRIFFIN   You couldn't stop them, you couldn't
get to Freddy?

REESE   I tried, I ran for him, but they were on him. I
couldn't reach him, the eight, nine of them were on
him—beating him, clawing him, tearing at his face.

FATHER GRIFFIN   Paul, you knew where I was. Why
didn't you call me?

REESE   There wasn't time! Even the kids on the other
side of the gym, they were running over and I yelled,
"Help me!"

DOBBS   You mean Freddy yelled.

REESE   No, *I yelled,* not Freddy. I yelled and these kids
who had run over grabbed me! Held me while the

others were on Freddy. And I heard somebody yell, "Hold that bastard!" and . . . and then I hit one of them . . . (*His voice catches*) . . . a couple of them— I don't know—and started to pull them off Freddy, who was crouching against the wall under them . . . pulled them off him. And Freddy, when I got to him, Freddy was covered with blood, coughing, spitting up blood. I raised his head, and when he saw me—God, I don't understand this, Freddy pushed himself against the wall, away from me, pushed himself away and screamed "NO!" *At me!* He was trying to get away from *me!* Trying to fight me off . . . until I grabbed him, lifted him up and . . . They didn't move, the other kids; just drew back . . . And I brought him . . . I didn't know where I was bringing him . . . God, God . . .

(*He stops, almost dazed. There is a pause.* FATHER MOZIAN *watches him, still unable to believe what he's heard.* REESE *gestures helplessly with both hands as he sits in* DOBBS' *chair at the table.* FATHER MOZIAN *gets up and paces*)

DOBBS   You brought him up here. You did the right thing.

REESE   He pulled away, he was fighting me! I swear it, Joe—he didn't want me to stop them!

DOBBS   Oh, come on Paul. That doesn't make sense. I know those boys.

REESE   Joe, I saw it.

DOBBS   What you saw was a schoolboy brawl, some kind of feud that just got out of hand.

FATHER MOZIAN   No, the boy obviously wanted to be hurt. There've been other incidents here the past few weeks; more and more violent, and senseless.

DOBBS   (*Still puzzled*)   Come on, Paul, I'll buy you a drink.

REESE (*Annoyed*)   No, Joe, I don't want a drink.

DOBBS   C'mon, it'll do you good.

> (FATHER MOZIAN *pulls a slip of paper from his folder and hands it to* REESE)

FATHER MOZIAN   Paul, is this all of them? Are those all the names?

REESE   Yes, Father.

DOBBS   What will you do to those boys?

FATHER MOZIAN (*To* FATHER GRIFFIN)   I don't know. How can I expel eleven boys?

DOBBS   Eleven? That's half a class.

FATHER MOZIAN (*To* FATHER GRIFFIN) Are they still in your office?

FATHER GRIFFIN Father Gerard's with them.

FATHER MOZIAN Send them back to their rooms for now. Wait for me in my office. (*Hands the list to* FATHER GRIFFIN) We'll decide what to do with them when I'm through here.

FATHER GRIFFIN (*To* DOBBS) Coming down, Joe?

DOBBS Paul, I'll wait for you downstairs. (*Turns out the lamp*) Father, I know those boys. I've taught every one of them. And if you want, I'll go down and talk to them and get this story straight. The boys always level with me.

FATHER MOZIAN Well, they'll have to level with me as well, Joe. Thanks anyway.

(DOBBS *leaves with* FATHER GRIFFIN. MALLEY *has put his coat on silently.* REESE *looks up as the door closes*)

FATHER MOZIAN Jerome, I'd like to talk to you before you go.

MALLEY (*Checking his watch*) The nurse leaves my mother at five. She shouldn't be alone.

FATHER MOZIAN   It won't take long. Paul?

REESE   I'm sorry, Father. The kids *liked* me.

FATHER MOZIAN   Paul, it's not your fault. There's nothing more you could have done. Go take Joe up on that drink and let me worry about this.

REESE   I've got to close the gym.

FATHER MOZIAN   Leave it for now.

REESE (*Getting his coat and bag*)   No, I want to go in there. There's got to be something I missed. Those kids wanted me to hit them. "Hold that bastard!" Crazy, but that hits me more than anything. Why'd they want to say that about me?

(*He leaves and exits into the gym*)

FATHER MOZIAN (*A pause*)   Jerome, about McArdle. What say we let him back in Thursday? I think two days is long enough.

MALLEY   The suspension was to be indefinite.

FATHER MOZIAN   That was before this incident. Besides, he's not a bad fellow from what I hear, and he's never been in serious trouble before this.

MALLEY He's had his champions, I'd imagine. Forgive me, Father, but this sort of leniency has a way of getting back to the boys.

FATHER MOZIAN Let it then. Maybe this sort of leniency is what we need right now. Sleep on it, all right?

MALLEY I don't foresee any changes overnight.

FATHER MOZIAN Sleep on it anyway. (*Pause*) How have they been for you in class lately, the boys?

MALLEY My students, I'm afraid, don't lend themselves to lengthy analysis.

FATHER MOZIAN Then you underestimate your students.

MALLEY If anything I'm being excessively charitable. They might spend more time on their Latin and less on their coiffures. That's hardly to the point, is it?

FATHER MOZIAN No, hardly. Jerome, are you aware of what's been going on in the classrooms? Some of the teachers seem to be losing any kind of control, especially the priests, and I'm not just talking about Father Penny.

MALLEY It's the teacher's role to enforce discipline, to insist on it. (*Pointedly*) And with the cooperation of the administration.

47

FATHER MOZIAN   Under ordinary circumstances, yes. But the classroom pranks have become more than pranks, more than adolescent defiance. What they're doing is deliberate and violent. *Why?*

MALLEY   I'm sure I don't know, Father.

FATHER MOZIAN   Jerome, it frightens me the way they've started going after one another. We've all got to try to understand what it is driving these boys. Maybe even revise our methods for a while.

(*He is watching* MALLEY, *trying to determine whether he's implied enough.* MALLEY *has been tense, distracted during the exchange; more so now*)

MALLEY   I'm too rough on them, is that it?

FATHER MOZIAN   If you put it that way, yes.

MALLEY   Why? Because I expect them to do a little work? For forty minutes a day, possibly even think?

FATHER MOZIAN   That's not what I'm talking about.

MALLEY   Then I don't know what you're talking about.

FATHER MOZIAN   Jerome, you've been here longer than I have, and that puts me in an awkward position.

MALLEY   Why should it? You're the headmaster.

(*They are standing at opposite ends of the room:* MALLEY *beside the door,* FATHER MOZIAN *next to the common table*)

FATHER MOZIAN   So I am. All right, everything right on the line. Jerome, I want you to ease up on those boys.

MALLEY   I see.

FATHER MOZIAN   Do you?

MALLEY   Perfectly. And perhaps you can suggest an appropriate pose as well. A friend, a chum . . .

FATHER MOZIAN   Please, don't make this any harder for me.

MALLEY   . . . a Mr. Dobbs—of course that's it—kindly, paternal!

FATHER MOZIAN   I'm not asking you to assume any kind of pose. All I'm saying is that we must all adjust to these peculiar circumstances.

MALLEY   (*A pause*)   No.

FATHER MOZIAN Jerome?

MALLEY No.

FATHER MOZIAN And that's final.

MALLEY That's final.

FATHER MOZIAN No, Jerome, I'm afraid it can't be final.

MALLEY (*Less controlled*) What is it you think I've been doing to these boys? I've been teaching here for ten years. My students have always been important to me. I wouldn't be here if that weren't true.

FATHER MOZIAN Jerome, I have great respect for you as a teacher, but I know your methods.

MALLEY You know what you've *heard* of my methods.

FATHER MOZIAN It's not what I've heard, it's what I've seen happening here that concerns me.

MALLEY What has that to do with me? My methods are not Dobbs' methods. Why must you judge me by him?

FATHER MOZIAN I am not judging you by Joe Dobbs.

MALLEY   I am paid to teach Latin and Greek. That's the extent of my responsibility to the school.

FATHER MOZIAN   And the human element?

MALLEY   I am not their chum! I will not tolerate laziness or stupidity, but I am not an ogre, not what Dobbs would have me!

FATHER MOZIAN   It's not what Dobbs would have you that concerns me. It's what the boys would have you. What they scrawl on the walls and pass to each other under the desks.

MALLEY   I'm not interested in what's written on the walls of a lavatory.

FATHER MOZIAN   Well, maybe you should be aware of it . . . the obscenity, the malevolence directed against you in this school.

MALLEY   Oh, I'm aware of it, the malevolence. I've been made aware of it . . .

FATHER MOZIAN   (*Moving toward him*) Are you? (*He takes a sheet of paper from his folder and holds it out to* MALLEY) Fully aware of it?

MALLEY   What is that?

FATHER MOZIAN   A note some of the boys were passing.

MALLEY   I'm not interested in notes.

FATHER MOZIAN   Read it, please.

> (MALLEY *takes the note, reads it slowly, and then crumples it*)

MALLEY   Where did you get this?

> (*Giving it back to* FATHER MOZIAN)

FATHER MOZIAN   That doesn't matter.

MALLEY   I have a right to know where this filth came from!

FATHER MOZIAN   That does not matter! What does matter is there've been other notes, uglier than that.

MALLEY   From whom? From what boys? I WANT THEIR NAMES!

FATHER MOZIAN   All of them directed against you. None of the other teachers, Jerome.

MALLEY   They wouldn't write such things about me . . . the boys.

FATHER MOZIAN I'm sorry for all of this, Jerome. But whether you like it or not, you must cooperate. There are two hundred boys in this school, and more than any of you, they're my responsibility.

MALLEY So he's reached you all, has he? As easily as he's reached those two hundred boys. (*Looking directly* at FATHER MOZIAN) *He's* the malevolence. *He's* the obscenity. (*Emphatically*) Dobbs wrote that note!

FATHER MOZIAN You actually believe that?

MALLEY I know it. I know what he's capable of.

FATHER MOZIAN What you're saying is *insane.* Jerome, I know what the boys think of you, I've seen the way they react to you.

MALLEY They react the way he's taught them to react. They're all his boys. This room is his . . . the school is his . . . everything here is his and it's all being used against me. (*Pointing to the note*) Dobbs wrote that note. There are no names, it was just handed to you. You know what I'm saying is true.

FATHER MOZIAN No, Jerome. I took the note from those boys.

MALLEY (*Shocked; shaking his head*) No, that's not

possible. (*He lists his schoolbag. He pulls open the door with a quick gesture. A slight catch in his voice*) That is not possible!

(*He leaves the room quickly, slamming the door behind him. The lights fade*)

Liturgical music is briefly heard as the lights come up on the chapel. The light is dim, reddish. On the wall is one of the Stations of the Cross in white marble: Christ falling beneath the weight of the cross. DOBBS *is standing in the rear of the chapel, behind a pew. He holds a string of rosary beads in one hand.* MALLEY *enters the chapel through the rear door, genuflects and moves into the pew. He kneels and buries his face in his hands.* DOBBS *watches him silently, the sound of the rosary beads hitting against the wooden pew.* MALLEY *becomes aware of his presence.*

MALLEY (*Whispers*) What are you doing here?

DOBBS I saw those boys, Jerome. I came in here to pray for them.

MALLEY Yes, Dobbs, you're a great comfort to all your boys.

DOBBS Well, who else have they got here but me? (*Putting the beads into his pocket, he pauses, looking straight ahead*) I remember, in grade school years ago, I re-

55

member the nuns telling us that God Himself was present on the altar whenever that small red light was burning. And how easy it was, in my child's mind, for the light itself to become God. I used to think . . . what if a wind were to blow into the church and find that light? Poof! . . . no more God? (*He gives a soft smile as he looks at the back of* MALLEY's *head*) Jerome, can we talk . . . calmly for once?

MALLEY (*Wearily*) I don't want to talk to you, Dobbs. Just leave me alone. You've all made your point, haven't you?

DOBBS I don't think so, no. Because you'll come in again tomorrow and it'll be the same pressure, the same going at the boys, all in the name of learning. They're children, Jerome.

MALLEY And I'm a teacher, nothing more than that. This school is my life.

DOBBS And mine as well.

MALLEY All I have is here. I'm a good teacher. I belong here.

DOBBS We all know that. If we're concerned—the headmaster, Father Griffin, all of us . . .

MALLEY It's for your boys, I know. The headmaster has made that very clear. As clear as you've made it to him.

DOBBS I've never said anything to him against you.

MALLEY I wouldn't expect the truth from you, Dobbs. Not even in here. (*Staring straight ahead*) The hate— the hate between us . . . How terrible, isn't it . . . that the two of us should find ourselves together here? Two such . . . second-rate human beings . . . two such empty lives . . . shackled together here.

DOBBS My life empty? With all I have here? (*Pauses; softly*) I don't hate you, Jerome.

MALLEY More, I think, than I hate you. All right, Dobbs, if it's finally to destroy one of us, then let it be just that—*one of us*. (*Half turns*) Listen to me. My mother is very ill.

DOBBS I know, Jerome, I know the strain you're under. Take it out on me if you have to, but leave the boys alone.

MALLEY (*More emphatic*) She's dying. I have no defense against that. If . . . I go along with you, if I try . . . will you at least have a little pity on her?

DOBBS Of course I pity her.

MALLEY You know what I'm talking about, don't you?

DOBBS I don't think I do.

MALLEY   There have been other calls besides McArdle's. Someone has been calling her. Terrible calls . . . terrible lies about me . . . Please, Dobbs, no more.

DOBBS   Do you know what you're saying to me?

MALLEY   I know exactly what I'm saying. For her sake, Dobbs—*no more!* I'll do whatever you want; whatever it does to me, I'll at least attempt it. But please leave her alone. Because you must know by now . . . there are kinder ways to destroy me.

(*He leans forward in the pew, covering his face with his hands.* DOBBS *makes a helpless gesture, then crosses himself and leaves the chapel slowly. There is a long pause.* MALLEY *is motionless. The light in the chapel has been growing redder. There is a movement then, very quiet, at the chapel's side door. A boy comes in and slips into the pew, staring straight ahead.* MALLEY *becomes aware of his presence. More movement: the rear door opens. Two more boys enter, supporting a third who is semiconscious. They stand directly behind* MALLEY *and wait.* MALLEY'S *hands fall from his face; he tries to see behind him. A pause; he gets up, lifts his schoolbag and leaves the pew without looking at the boys around him. He leaves the chapel. As soon as he does, the semiconscious boy collapses over the back of the pew. The boys press close to him now and tear off his jacket, exposing his whiplashed back. He moans as they raise him up and hang him by his wrists from the cross hanging on the wall. They leave the chapel quickly. The boy does not make a sound now. The chapel bells begin to ring. After a few moments,* FATHER MOZIAN *enters from the rear door, crosses himself and kneels in the pew. The bells continue to ring.* FATHER GRIFFIN *follows him in; as he genuflects, the boy moans loudly. They turn toward the sound)*

FATHER GRIFFIN *(Rushing toward the boy)*   Dear God! Frank! Frank, help me! What are they doing, what are they—?

(They lift the boy from the cross and cradle him with his head resting on the back of the pew)

FATHER MOZIAN *(Voice rising)*   I want this chapel closed!

(The bells are growing louder)

FATHER GRIFFIN   It's the chapel, Frank, you can't close the chapel!

FATHER MOZIAN   I said lock it! *Lock it, lock it!*

(His voice is covered by the sound of the bells. The red light goes out)

59

SCENE FOUR

The lights come up in the Faculty Room. DOBBS *is handing* SHEA, *a senior, composition books.*

DOBBS   I appreciate the help, Shea.

SHEA   It's nothing, sir.

DOBBS *(A little breathless)*   Try not to grow old, boy. The body's not built to take it. *(Handing him the last of the books)* There you go. Put those on the table and count them. Should be thirty of 'em. *(*SHEA *puts the books on the table.* DOBBS *is looking for an opening)* Shea? *(*SHEA *stops counting)* I want you to give it to me straight now: What happened in the chapel yesterday?

*(*SHEA *goes back to counting)*

SHEA *(Tonelessly)*   I don't know anything about it, sir.

DOBBS   That may be a good enough answer for the headmaster and Father Griffin; this is Mr. Dobbs asking.

You do know a boy was beaten up and left in the chapel. I want you to tell me how something so terrible could happen here.

SHEA I don't know, sir. I wasn't there.

DOBBS I'm not saying you were. I don't want any names. I just want to know why any boys in this school would desecrate their own chapel.

(FATHER GRIFFIN *enters the room and sees* SHEA)

FATHER GRIFFIN Shea, what are you doing in here?

DOBBS He's helping me, Father.

FATHER GRIFFIN Where's your next class?

SHEA Library.

FATHER GRIFFIN Are you finished with him, Mr. Dobbs?

DOBBS I don't know. Am I, Shea?

SHEA (*Very clearly*) Yes, sir.

(*He starts to pick up his books*)

DOBBS (*Stopping* SHEA) Are you sure? (SHEA *nods*) Okay. Put them on the desk in 1C.

(*The class bell rings.* SHEA *starts for the door*)

FATHER GRIFFIN Shea, three minutes. You've got three minutes to deliver those books and get to class.

(SHEA *leaves and goes down the stairs as* REESE *enters from the gym*)

DOBBS Morning, Paul.

REESE Morning.

DOBBS Father, I hope you're bringing us some good news this morning.

FATHER GRIFFIN I'm afraid not, Joe. We're canceling all masses and services in the school till further notice.

DOBBS You can't be serious. Father, the boys need to feel the presence of God more than ever now. I don't have to tell you that.

FATHER GRIFFIN I'm very serious, Joe. (*Checks his clipboard*) All students will report to their home rooms for study during the chapel period. You hear that, Paul?

REESE   I'm afraid I did.

FATHER GRIFFIN   Well, I've got a little more for you. (*Reads*) The school building is closed immediately after the last period.

DOBBS   You're locking the kids out of the building, locking . . . God out of the building.

FATHER GRIFFIN   Any boy found in the building after three-fifteen is on suspension.

DOBBS   Father, there was no faculty meeting on this. I wasn't consulted.

FATHER GRIFFIN   That's straight from the headmaster's office, Joe.

DOBBS   What about my conferences with the boys?

FATHER GRIFFIN   You're going to have to take that up with him.

DOBBS   I will, Father. I will.

REESE   I suppose that knocks out intramurals?

FATHER GRIFFIN   It knocks out all extracurriculars. And, Paul, the gym is out of bounds except for gym classes.

DOBBS   Father, wait a minute . . .

FATHER GRIFFIN   Joe, Frank is headmaster. This is the way he wants to handle the situation. (DOBBS *shrugs and moves away*) I'm sorry.

DOBBS   So am I, so am I.

(FATHER GRIFFIN *leaves and goes downstairs*)

REESE   Fifteen minutes to get out of the building. If he's running that scared, why open it at all?

DOBBS   Don't worry about it, young man. I've been in this school thirty years. No boy has ever held anything back from me in all that time, and I don't intend for it to start now.

(*The class bell rings.* DOBBS *leaves the room angrily and goes down the stairs.* REESE *is setting his books up on the table. Two boys come up the stairs stealthily. One moves ahead to check that the way is clear. He signals to the other. They continue up and stop in the middle of the staircase. One of the boys is carrying a red markbook. He takes careful aim and throws it against the Faculty Room door. Both run up the stairs and disappear.* REESE *rushes to the door, opens it, and picks up the book and the scattered papers. As he puts them together, he notices something scrawled in the markbook. A look of distaste crosses his face as he rips the page from the book and crumples it.* MALLEY *is coming down the stairs now, slowly, uncertainly.* REESE *moves back to the table, deciding what to do with the torn-out page. He slips it into his pocket as* MALLEY *enters the room. A bit rattled,* REESE *holds the book out to him)*

REESE   Here's your markbook, Mr. Malley.

MALLEY *(Going to him)*   My markbook? Where did you get that?

REESE   Found it . . . outside. You must've dropped it.

(MALLEY takes the book and checks it, trying to remember)

MALLEY   How could I have done that? I had it in my last class; I'm sure I did.

REESE   Me, I'm always forgetting things.

(Looks quickly at MALLEY, who hasn't heard him)

MALLEY   I never go to class without my markbook.

(He goes to the alcove)

65

REESE   I gave back a history test once and forgot all about recording the marks.

MALLEY   (*Still trying to figure it out*)   I've never done that before.

REESE   Joe told me to bluff it—tell them I wanted to look over one of the essay questions again. Boy, did they see through that! (*Sees that* MALLEY *isn't listening; his voice trails off*) Guess Joe can . . . hand them a better line.

(MALLEY *looks up, not exactly at* REESE)

MALLEY   Just now . . . I found myself walking through the halls . . . I don't think I knew where I was going.

REESE   Sir?

MALLEY   (*With difficulty, trying to explain it more to himself. Sitting*)   After my last class . . . What could have come over me . . . to wander through the halls that way? I lost my way. (*Convincing himself*) I didn't know what I was doing!

REESE   (*Hand extended*)   Can I . . . Is there anything I can do?

MALLEY   What happened to me?

REESE (*Moves toward the door*)   I'll get Joe.

MALLEY   No! Nobody. I'll be all right.

(*He tries to compose himself.* REESE *watches him with great concern*)

REESE   Are you sure?

MALLEY (*Hand on his markbook again*)   I *know* I had this in class with me.

(*Aware of* REESE's *stare, he starts flipping through some papers*)

REESE   Look, Mr. Malley, are you all right?

MALLEY (*Speaks without looking up*)   I'd be thankful if you could forget all about this . . . stupid episode. It was inexcusable of me.

REESE (*Moving toward him*)   You don't have to apologize.

MALLEY   I'm not apologizing! I . . . blacked out, that's all. I've been under a great strain lately.

REESE   I know. Your mother.

MALLEY Yes. My mother. (*With difficulty*) Her condition is much worse the last few days.

REESE I'm sorry to hear that. That's rough on top of everything else. Look, if there's anything I can do . . .

(FATHER GRIFFIN *is coming down the stairs quickly. He opens the Faculty Room door; looks in*)

FATHER GRIFFIN Is George Penny in here?

REESE No, he's not, Father.

(FATHER PENNY *runs up the staircase*)

FATHER GRIFFIN Well, if he comes in, will you tell him . . . (*He hears* FATHER PENNY, *turns and calls loudly*) . . . 2C is waiting for him to teach biology.

FATHER PENNY (*Breathless*) Sorry. I was in levitation and I couldn't get down.

(FATHER PENNY *continues up the stairs*)

FATHER GRIFFIN What does it take to make that guy sober up?

(*He leaves, down the stairs*)

REESE (*After a pause; peering at* MALLEY'S *papers*)   Test, hunh?

MALLEY (*Uncomfortable, aware of* REESE)   No. Composition. Caesar.

REESE   Caesar . . . (*Thinks hard; starts to recite*) *Gallia est omni divida . . . in tres . . . partes . . .*

MALLEY   . . . *omnis divisa in partes tres.*

REESE (*Abashed; smiles*)   You probably remember what a brain I was in Latin 2. The old 2B. I was the clod in the last seat near the window. That seems like such a helluva long time ago—nine years. (*With great effort*) A lot can happen in nine years. I have been trying, you know? To fit in here.

MALLEY   And now you're apologizing to me? (*Looks up*) Why?

REESE   Because I'm afraid you don't have much respect for me as a teacher.

MALLEY   Does what I think of you really matter?

REESE   Well, yes. I mean . . . we're sort of . . . colleagues.

(*The word comes out with difficulty*)

MALLEY   Yes, I suppose, we are . . . colleagues. And it's time we came to grips with that.

REESE   Yeah, because . . . I'm afraid of you. Isn't that something? So it's important to me just to work up enough courage to talk to you like this. I hate like hell to have to hide in the john every time we have a free period together.

MALLEY   I'm sorry I make you so uncomfortable.

REESE   It's not you, Lash, it's me.

(*He grimaces; waits for an explosion*)

MALLEY   (*A quick look*)   Afraid of me.

REESE   *Still.*

MALLEY   Well, why not? I'm frightening, a menacing figure. I'm sure you've heard that over and over. Coupled with your own memories of my classroom . . . tyranny. I'm sure that's all been refreshed for you.

REESE   (*Defeated*)   I'm sorry. (*Gathers his books*)   I'll get out of your way now. I'll work in the gym.

(*He gets up and heads for the door.* MALLEY *raises one hand*)

MALLEY   No, *wait!* (*Just to say something*) You . . . stay around late, do you?

REESE (*Stops*)   Yes, I do. Often. Stay late.

MALLEY (*Nods; can't pursue it*)   A singularly stupid class, wasn't it, your old 2B?

REESE   The worst.

MALLEY   The worst. I have a newspaper clipping somewhere. That was your 2B, wasn't it?

REESE (*Moving back into the room*)   Yeah.

MALLEY   Yes. You boys had left it on the desk for me.

REESE   You weren't too happy about it.

MALLEY   Someday I must look for that clipping; something about . . .

REESE (*Very cautiously*)   A student stabbing his teacher.

MALLEY   Ah, yes, I remember feeling vaguely threatened at the time.

(REESE *puts down his books, and moves toward the refrigerator*)

REESE (*Tentative*) Would you like a Coke?

MALLEY (*A few seconds to absorb the offer*) Thank you, I have some tea. (*He gets up and goes to his schoolbag. Takes out a thermos and pours himself a cup of tea*) That became a famous incident among you boys, didn't it? Something to add to the Lash catalogue of infamy.

REESE (*Sitting at the table*) You had us all kneeling in the aisle.

MALLEY Did I?

REESE Forty minutes.

MALLEY (*Drinking his tea and moving out of the alcove toward* REESE) I imagine . . . that's the sort of reminiscing you do when you boys get together.

REESE Oh, yeah.

MALLEY Do you keep in touch?

REESE Sometimes.

MALLEY Dwyer . . . do you ever see him?

REESE Not since graduation, no.

MALLEY Dirty fingernails, but a first-rate mind, one of the best I've ever taught. And Peter Jackmin?

REESE He's still in the seminary.

MALLEY He may actually pick up a bit of Latin. It was Jackmin who put the clipping on my desk.

REESE (*Surprised*) You knew that?

MALLEY Not then. I had a Christmas card from him once, with a note. Sometimes I hear from you boys . . . after a while. More than you'd think. (*Moves over to the alcove table with his thermos*) A singularly stupid class; a trying year—like all of them, I suppose. You boys are afraid of me, I know. Maybe I am too hard on you. Maybe I shouldn't be teaching, at least not in a high school. It's not that I dislike you. It's just that . . . you're children, and some of you are so slow. I don't have much patience with the slow ones. (*Pause*) You'll find that . . . the pattern of one's life can be formed so suddenly, without realizing it. So suddenly and, for some of us, so irrevocably. And if it's wrong? Well, one comes in and goes through the motions, thinking at first that next year will be different . . . and realizing gradually that, no, next year will be the same and the year after that and, well, if that's the way it's to be . . . that's the way it's to be. And so . . . I save newspaper clippings and Christmas cards. Why do I save them? I don't know. But wouldn't it be comforting some day to take out all those bits of the past and lay them out on the floor like paths through a maze, and see what the course of my life has been . . . perhaps see what's been there all along, tucked away in a drawer? (*Pause*) If I've hurt you, any of you boys, I'm sorry . . . but that's what I am . . . (*Pause. The phone rings*) . . . that's the only way I know . . . (*Pause. The phone rings again.* MALLEY *stops and looks at it.* REESE *has been standing, absorbed in* MALLEY'S *sudden opening up to him. The ringing breaks his concentration.* REESE *sees that* MALLEY, *who is closer to the phone, will not answer it.* MALLEY *stares at the phone, his expression darkening.* REESE *moves toward the phone quietly*) No! . . . Don't answer it! I won't speak to him!

(REESE *looks at him as the phone rings. No movement; the phone keeps ringing*)

REESE   Maybe I better . . . ? (REESE'S *hand is on the receiver, and his eyes on* MALLEY. *He lifts the receiver*) Mr. Reese . . . (*To* MALLEY) It's for you . . . Mrs. Carter . . . Your mother's nurse?

(MALLEY *takes the receiver and holds it for a moment without speaking.* REESE *is watching him*)

MALLEY   Yes . . . I see . . . All right . . . Yes . . . (*Pause; then the barest whisper*) All right . . . Thank you . . .

(*Slowly he lowers the receiver to the table. No movement for several moments. He seems unaware of* REESE's *stare as he goes to the closet for his coat, and then slowly walks toward the door*)

REESE Jerome? (MALLEY *looks at him and begins to weep.* REESE *takes a step toward him; his hand moves in a helpless quieting motion. He seems near tears himself now*)

MALLEY (*At the door, holding it open*) It's just that . . . I should have been with her . . . for that . . .

(*He goes out into the corridor and down the stairs.* REESE *remains motionless as the lights fade*)

It is evening, three days later. The lighting is dim. REESE *is at the ditto machine on the balcony. A boy is moving up the stairs from the lower floor. He stops at the landing, listening for sounds from the Faculty Room. He is about to go up to the next floor when distant laughter is heard from the dining hall downstairs. He goes down the corridor quickly, toward the gym area.*

Now there is silence. FATHER PENNY, *glass in hand, is climbing the stairs. He starts for the Faculty Room, and stops as he sees the statue atop the newel post.*

FATHER PENNY (*Addressing the statue*) What's a nice saint like you . . . ? (*He leaves it incomplete, and moves —just a bit unsteadily—into the Faculty Room. He sees* REESE) Ah! There you are. Ten o'clock and nothing's well. You're missing the high point of the faculty meeting—the booze.

(*He holds up the glass*)

REESE (*With little interest*) Everybody still down there?

FATHER PENNY Oh, yes. The faculty, having met in extraordinary session, has dragged its collective ass to the dining hall, where they are raising their glasses like a wall against the plague. The feeling seems to be: we survived the Colosseum, we'll survive this blood bath. We are dancing on the ruins.

(*He does a quick soft-shoe*)

REESE (*Looking down*) George, George—I don't think I'm ready for that tonight.

FATHER PENNY Don't you go sour on me too. I came up here to get away from all those craggy faces farting around down there. (*Sits in* DOBBS' *chair*) Isn't that why you sneaked away?

REESE I had a history test to run off.

FATHER PENNY Anybody left to take it?

(*He laughs rowdily, then beats his breast in expiation*)

REESE Nice to know there are some twisted minds left.

(*He starts to come down to the lower level. Noise is heard from below: voices raised, some laughter*)

FATHER PENNY   Ah! Father Headmaster has pinned the tail on the donkey.

(*He rises and dances quickly, professionally, across the room*)

REESE (*At the table now*)   Very smooth. (FATHER PENNY *falls over the arm of* DOBBS' *chair*)

FATHER PENNY   Thank you. One never knows where liturgical reform will lead.

REESE   George? You ever think of going over the wall?

FATHER PENNY   All the time.

REESE   I was only kidding.

FATHER PENNY   I wasn't.

REESE   You're a bad influence on me, George.

FATHER PENNY (*Touching his cassock*)   Don't be put off by the cassock. Its sanctity is becoming one of the great mysteries of faith. In view of what's happening around here, it dwarfs the Immaculate Conception. (*Getting up*) Come on downstairs with me; we'll shake them up.

REESE (*Packing his schoolbag*) I'm going home.

FATHER PENNY Father Headmaster will be displeased.

REESE Tough shit.

FATHER PENNY Ah, spunk! You may make it out of here yet.

REESE Sorry, George, this place is beginning to get to me.

FATHER PENNY (*Sitting in* MALLEY's *chair at the table*) Don't know why you say that. Chapel sealed, boys flagellating themselves—happens in the best of cloisters. But we're not to think of that tonight. Orders from On High. None of us may make it out of here alive, but tonight we're . . . *having fun.* Someone dropped a glass a few minutes ago and we all reached for our rosaries. (*He makes a quick "rosary" motion, and begins to sing dissonantly*) You're telling your beads more than you're telling me . . .

(*He chuckles again*)

REESE (*More seriously now*) You wouldn't really go over the wall, would you?

FATHER PENNY (*Pause*) I have taken vows. (*Getting up*) May I use the lay toilets? The urinals downstairs have suspicious wires running from the flushers. (*Moves toward the lavatory*) I shall be blown up decorously or not at all.

REESE   Don't write on the walls.

FATHER PENNY   I'll leave that to the already moving finger.

> (*He goes into the lavatory.* REESE *takes his canvas bag to the table, and begins to pack up. A soft, wordless moan comes from the stairwell, then a distinct "no," followed by whispering. A boy comes up the stairs, his back against the rail. A second boy pursues slowly in the middle of the stairs, his arms extended to prevent the first boy's escape. A third boy comes from the gym and stops at the top of the stairs as the first boy reaches the landing and starts to back down to the right. Another boy has appeared at the head of the stairs. He comes down quickly and grabs the first boy, putting his hand over his mouth. One of the other boys punches him in the stomach; the victim doubles over. The boys drag him up the stairs.* REESE *moves slowly toward the door as the sounds build in the hallway. He opens the Faculty Room door, and moves slowly out into the corridor. There is silence; the boys have disappeared.* REESE *goes back into the Faculty Room and closes the door as* FATHER PENNY *comes out of the lavatory*)

FATHER PENNY   What's wrong?

REESE I think there are kids in the building.

FATHER PENNY It's after ten. They've all been flushed back to their rooms.

REESE I know I heard them a minute ago.

FATHER PENNY (*Tries to pass it off*) Well, *I've* had a revelation in the terlet! The boys are clearly possessed. Which means we need an exorcist and a herd of swine, fast.

REESE Something's wrong with those kids. I'm sure they're in the building.

FATHER PENNY Well, I'm sure about that possession idea. (*Touching his cassock, serious now*) This might have been the wrong way for me to go . . . but I believe in God, and I believe in Satan. (*Pauses; looks at his glass*) And now I believe I'll go have another drink.

REESE Be careful, George.

FATHER PENNY On second thought, I'll go back to the reliquary. (*Handing his glass to* REESE) A little free advice? You haven't taken vows. Why don't you get out of here?

REESE I don't want to get out of here. I want to be a teacher.

FATHER PENNY   Be one somewhere else. You don't want
to turn into one of those dried-up old celibates down
there, clacking their beads and their teeth. That's my
role.

(FATHER PENNY *leaves the room, and goes back
down the stairs quickly.* REESE *closes the door after
him. He looks at the glass* FATHER PENNY *has
handed him, thinks a moment; he seems to dismiss
a thought. He throws the glass into the wastebasket. The glass shatters. Two more boys have
come quietly into the corridor, from the gym area.
They stop at the sound of the glass breaking. One
of them turns front, the light on his face. He waits
for something, his companion watching him.* REESE
*is looking at the broken glass in the wastebasket.
He bends slowly and retrieves a piece of it. The
boy in the corridor tenses, leaning against the newel
post.* REESE *rises, and opens his palm; he looks
from his hand to the glass. He brings the glass to
his hand slowly. The boy in the hall moans softly
and closes his eyes. A pause, and then* REESE
presses the jagged edge into his palm. REESE *and
the boy cry out in pain at the same time.* REESE
*bends forward, covering his bleeding hand with
the uninjured one. The second boy has grabbed the
first; he leads him up the stairs.* REESE *grabs a towel
from the rack beside the refrigerator, and wraps it
around his hand. His back is to the Faculty Room
door as he bites his lip, waiting for the pain to pass.
There is a long pause.* DOBBS *comes up the stairs
and enters the Faculty Room*)

REESE (*Turns quickly at the sound*) Jesus, Joe, creep up on me like that.

DOBBS (*His mind back downstairs*) Those black robes think they know it all. They'll handle it their way. Well, their way is making it impossible for me to talk to my boys. They're frightening the boys. That's why those boys are avoiding me. (*Notices* REESE's *hand*) What's wrong with your hand?

REESE I cut myself.

DOBBS Well, the doctor just happens to be in. Sit down there.

REESE It's all right.

DOBBS Sit down, sit down. (REESE *sits in* MALLEY's *chair while* DOBBS *takes the first-aid kit from a shelf*) I've patched torn hands, knees, elbows, trousers. Been doing it for years. Everything needed to repair an adolescent boy is somewhere in this room.

REESE (*Impatient*) I'm not an adolescent boy.

DOBBS You're still a freshman to me, young man. You just got your growth a little faster than the other boys. You're all freshmen to me, whatever you go on to when you leave the old man. Doctors, bishops, councilmen

—what do I care? I knew them when their faces were changing. Hold still.

(DOBBS *touches* REESE's *hand.* REESE *pulls away*)

REESE   Leave it alone, hunh?

DOBBS   Come on, boy. (*Takes* REESE's *hand again and begins to bandage the cut*) How'd you manage this?

REESE   I cut myself.

DOBBS   I'm asking how you did it.

REESE   Joe . . . I did it deliberately.

DOBBS   What do you mean, deliberately?

REESE   Just what I said. I broke a glass and cut myself deliberately.

DOBBS   You don't cut yourself deliberately. When we cut ourselves we call that an accident. Now you can all put that in your notebooks.

REESE   Joe, I don't understand. Why would I want to hurt myself? Why? What's in this building that made me want to hurt myself?

DOBBS   All right, Paul, you cut yourself. Now let's leave it at that.

REESE   That's not enough.

DOBBS   Well, it'll just have to be enough for now. You're too excitable, boy. I meant to tell you that downstairs.

REESE   Why, because I got pissed off at that meeting? Let me tell you something, Joe. Your friends downstairs are panicking. They're just looking for a scapegoat. Something's gone wrong in this school and you're all looking for something to pin it on and it looks like you've all elected Jerome.

DOBBS   Nobody says it's just Jerome.

REESE   Well, you were all sure hinting at it.

DOBBS   If I remember correctly, there was a time when you were afraid to be in the same room with—*Jerome*.

REESE   Well, maybe that was my fault more than his. We talked for the first time . . . just before he got the call about his mother. Did I tell you that?

DOBBS   (*More slowly*)   No. And what was it you talked about—Jerome and you?

REESE I don't know—just talked. Joe, he's different, changed. You didn't see him at the funeral this morning.

DOBBS I had a class.

REESE Well, you should have seen him. He's not the same person. If it means anything, he's not here now; he hasn't been anywhere near the place for three days. And I'm still afraid. Whatever there is in this building is in here now. And Joe . . . the kids are in here.

DOBBS The boys? In here?

REESE I know they're in here. I heard them. Why, Joe? What do they want in here? What are they looking for?

DOBBS You're sure full of questions tonight, young man.

REESE Well, nobody around here's been coming up with any answers. What about you, old man? You've always had them. All right, why are the kids in the building now?

DOBBS They're not in the building!

REESE They are, for Chrissake!

DOBBS They're not! I'd know it if they were. I'll show you. (*He gets up, crosses out into the corridor and goes halfway up the stairs. When he speaks, it is almost a litany)* Bassman? Blake? Curran? DeLeo? Enright? Hartnett? Keaney? Kearney? Landis? Martin? Sheppard? Tapken? *(Starts back down the stairs)* Uzzo? Weeks? *(Stops, meditative)* And Bennie Zeller . . . English 1D. Nineteen fifty-two. Nobody there . . . *(He stands beside the statue.* REESE *has come out into the corridor.* DOBBS *looks at him, his eyes suddenly glazed, distant)* I've taught over two thousand boys, do you know that? Other men's sons, two thousand of them. I've always valued it, the affection of all those boys, their friendship . . . years of it. You know me, you boys. It's you, you I trust. Not myself, but you, all those boys. And what you see, what all those boys have seen in me, that must be what I am . . . truly, isn't that so? This is my school. I've spent thirty years in this building . . . And what you see is all there is. There's nothing to frighten you.

REESE   I *am* scared, Joe. This place scares the hell out of me.

DOBBS   It's just a school, for God's sake.

REESE   I know it's just a school. I went here. *(DOBBS moves in front of REESE and goes back into the Faculty Room. REESE follows, closing the door)* I know every room and every corridor. I can take you downstairs and show you my old desk, my locker; but it changed. It's not the same. Something's come into this place.

DOBBS   Your imagination, that's what.

87

REESE No, Joe, it's not my imagination. It's something real. It's real enough to touch. (*He holds up his hand, and looks at it, as if realizing something for the first time*) And I touched it. *I touched it.* (*There is a shrill scream from the offstage corridor upstairs. The victim the boys had selected is pushed out into the corridor. He stumbles down the top steps, and flails about for the bannister to break his fall. The boy's glasses have been shattered; his eyes are bloody. He feels his way down the remaining steps as* DOBBS *and* REESE *rush out into the hall.* DOBBS *grabs the boy as* REESE *stops suddenly, too shocked to move. The boy pulls away from* DOBBS *and falls against* REESE, *whose arms go around him*)

REESE (*Almost inaudibly*) God . . . his eyes . . . his . . .

(*He lifts the boy and begins to carry him down the stairs.* DOBBS' *hands reach out helplessly. Faculty voices are heard again from downstairs—louder, more jovial now. The lights fade*)

SCENE SIX

The lights come up. A boy is coming from the gym, another from the floor below. Both look, almost instinctively, toward the Faculty Room, for just a moment, then continue. They meet beside the statue on the newel post, exchange a look without speaking, and then continue. The first boy descends the stairs, the second boy continues up. FATHER GRIFFIN *has appeared at the head of the stairs. He stops and watches the boys. The second boy passes him without seeing him.* FATHER GRIFFIN *has stepped aside to let the boy pass. After a pause,* FATHER GRIFFIN *continues down.*

When he reaches the landing he stops; someone else is coming up. He waits. It is MALLEY, *climbing slowly, his eyes downcast. His expression, when he looks up at* FATHER GRIFFIN, *is one of profound weariness.*

FATHER GRIFFIN (*Seeing the change in him*) Jerome. Why have you come back so soon? We told you to stay out the whole week.

MALLEY Three days were enough. You were a great help to me yesterday at the funeral, Father. Thank you. I had hoped more of the priests would have come.

89

FATHER GRIFFIN (*Very gently*) Go home now, Jerome.

MALLEY No, Father. I have a class.

FATHER GRIFFIN I don't think that's wise.

MALLEY I'm all right now. Thank you.

(*He enters the Faculty Room.* FATHER GRIFFIN *looks after him as* FATHER MOZIAN *comes up the stairs. During the following,* MALLEY *takes off his coat and goes through his routine activity, almost numbly, preparing for the class*)

FATHER GRIFFIN Frank . . .

FATHER MOZIAN (*His voice low and troubled, before* FATHER GRIFFIN *can say more*) I know, Bill, I saw him.

FATHER GRIFFIN Then go easy on him, hunh?

FATHER MOZIAN I only wish I could. Make sure his classes are being covered. And there's to be a general assembly second period. Please see that it's announced. (FATHER GRIFFIN *goes up the stairs, and* FATHER MOZIAN *enters the Faculty Room quietly*) Jerome . . .

MALLEY Good morning, Father.

FATHER MOZIAN (*Watching him*) I hardly expected to see you here today, Jerome.

MALLEY (*Busy with books*) I know, but it's better for me this way.

FATHER MOZIAN Your classes are being covered.

MALLEY There's no need for that.

FATHER MOZIAN Father Brooke's been reassigned to second-year Latin. I'll handle your Greek class myself.

MALLEY I've never had another teacher take my classes. A week without me and they'll forget everything.

FATHER MOZIAN That's not our major concern right now.

MALLEY If this is still a school, then it should be. The boys are lazy, you've got to keep at them.

(*He crosses up to the alcove for a pencil*)

FATHER MOZIAN (*Pauses; as gently as possible*) The new assignments are permanent, Jerome.

MALLEY Permanent?

FATHER MOZIAN As of first period today. Jerome, this is very painful for me.

MALLEY Then please, don't. There's no need, there's . . . I've thought it over . . . and of course you're right. I'll change my methods . . .

FATHER MOZIAN Jerome, I'm afraid that doesn't matter now.

MALLEY If you'll just give me a little time to get my thoughts in order . . . I'll explain . . . I can revise the course . . . we can discuss that . . .

FATHER MOZIAN There's nothing to discuss. I know what you've been through the past few days . . .

MALLEY You don't. You wouldn't be saying this to me now if that were true. I . . . won't be dismissed. I'll do whatever you say, I'll go against what I believe, but I won't be dismissed. Not for something I'm not responsible for. Not from this school. And please, not now. I'll change my methods . . .

FATHER MOZIAN (*Taking an envelope from his leather folder*) This is addressed to you. You know what it is?

(MALLEY *takes a long look at the envelope*)

MALLEY (*Almost inaudibly*) Yes.

FATHER MOZIAN Have you received them before?

MALLEY (*Same*) Yes.

FATHER MOZIAN Pictures like this? . . . You're teaching young boys, Jerome.

MALLEY (*Very slowly, painfully*) Whatever there is in my life, I have never brought it into this school.

FATHER MOZIAN Well, I'm afraid it *has* come into the school now. How long have you been getting this kind of thing here?

MALLEY Here? Never.

FATHER MOZIAN Jerome, there's no point in lying to me.

MALLEY No, never here. At my home, yes, but not here. But I should have expected that, shouldn't I? That's why Father Griffin was so concerned about me. I imagine it's all over the faculty by now. Mr. Malley is, after all, just another dirty joke. Has it been passed down to the students yet?

FATHER MOZIAN I'm sorry, Jerome. You do understand my position?

(*He places the envelope back in his folder*)

MALLEY (*Thinking; his hands moving nervously*) Yes, yes, of course I do. (FATHER MOZIAN *starts to leave*) Wait! Father . . . ? (*Trying to control himself as he moves toward* FATHER MOZIAN) Try to understand mine. Those pictures are being sent to me. Deliberately sent to me.

FATHER MOZIAN (*Has stopped*)   Sent to you?

MALLEY   Yes. I have nothing to do with them.

FATHER MOZIAN   They're addressed to you. You've involved the school—all of us—in this.

MALLEY   I've tried to stop them. I have always destroyed them. You must believe that.

FATHER MOZIAN   Jerome, I have no other choice. You admit you've received them before.

MALLEY (*More desperate*)   But they're being *sent* to me! Don't you understand?

FATHER MOZIAN (*Challenging; he knows*)   Sent to you by whom, Jerome?

MALLEY   You'd believe me? You'd believe that such deliberate . . . malevolence could be directed at me by . . . Dobbs? Dobbs?

FATHER MOZIAN (*Pause. Directly at him*) No, Jerome.

MALLEY And if it's the truth?

FATHER MOZIAN Then it's a truth I can't afford to face. Not now, Jerome, not with everything else I've got to face here. And we both know that something like that cannot be true. Don't we?

MALLEY Of course you're right. How could it be so easy to select a victim . . . and turn everything against him?

FATHER MOZIAN I cannot afford something like this now, Jerome. Please, let's end it!

MALLEY End it. And how easily it solves the problem of Mr. Malley. Anything would have worked, wouldn't it?

FATHER MOZIAN (*Harder*) I think it would be best if you left this school as soon as possible.

MALLEY Best for whom?

FATHER MOZIAN For all of us.

MALLEY *No!* How can I make you understand it's true? *He is destroying me!* My mother first, and now me. There must be some way I can make you understand that what is happening to me is true. He can't win this easily, can he?

FATHER MOZIAN (*A step away*) I'm sorry, Jerome.

MALLEY Wait! You're a priest, before everything you're a priest. If I got down on my knees to you . . . would you believe me?

(*He is beside him*)

FATHER MOZIAN (*Moving away further*) That's enough, please!

MALLEY If I were to humiliate myself before you . . . make my confession to you . . . then you'd have to believe me . . . (*Falls to his knees before* FATHER MOZIAN) Bless me, Father, bless me for I have sinned . . .

FATHER MOZIAN (*Pulling away*) I said that's enough!

MALLEY (*Overwhelmed*) But you're a priest! You can't deny me confession, not if you're a priest—

FATHER MOZIAN (*His back to him*) You're contract with this school is terminated. (*Turns to him. Voice quavering*) And I forbid you, I absolutely forbid you to go up to those boys.

(*He leaves the room quickly*)

MALLEY (*Still on his knees*) Then . . . what are you . . . all of you?

(*He pulls himself up, very slowly. Looks around the room and then moves, almost blindly, toward the table. He picks up his books and walks out into the corridor, leaving the Faculty Room door open. He stops beside the staircase, suddenly unsure of his direction. The class bell rings, like a blow against his brain. He is motionless now.* REESE *is coming up the stairs. He sees* MALLEY *immediately*)

REESE Jerome? (*Reaching out for him*) Come into the Faculty Room.

MALLEY I have a class.

REESE No, you can't go up like this. Come and sit down for a while.

(*He leads* MALLEY *toward the Faculty Room*)

MALLEY I told you I have a class!

REESE All right, later.

(*Seating* MALLEY. MALLEY *grabs* REESE's *arm*)

MALLEY Now. Second period. There's no way he can stop me. I'm not responsible, not for any of it. He's a priest before everything; and if I tell him that again,

if I explain everything to him when my mind is clearer,
when I can think more clearly . . . then he's got to
believe me. Because it's the truth, all of it is true.

REESE (*Bending before him*) Jerome, I can't follow you,
I don't understand what you're saying. Let me get somebody—

MALLEY *There is nobody!* Paul . . . there was no need
. . . no reason to torment her like that . . . an old
woman who was dying . . . my mother. He was sending
those pictures to my home. He was calling her, telling
her lies about me, destroying her with those terrible
lies . . . All of it deliberate. And I don't understand, I
don't understand why he's doing this to me!

REESE What calls? Who was calling?

MALLEY *Dobbs. Dobbs.*

REESE Joe? . . . Jerome, I don't know what you're saying.

MALLEY How could I protect myself against someone
like that? Someone who could know me so completely?
What defense do I have against so much hate?

(DOBBS *comes down the corridor and opens the
Faculty Room door*)

DOBBS (*A long look. Slowly*) What are you doing here,
Jerome?

Pat Hingle as JOSEPH DOBBS, Ken Howard as
PAUL REESE and Fritz Weaver as JEROME
MALLEY.

REESE He was going upstairs and I brought him in here . . .

DOBBS You don't belong in this school, Jerome.

MALLEY It's all yours now, Dobbs, isn't it?

REESE What do you mean, he doesn't belong in this school?

(*Standing up beside* MALLEY's *chair*)

DOBBS Just what I said.

MALLEY It's taken you ten years, but you've won.

DOBBS (*To* REESE) What's he been telling you?

REESE (*Challenging*) I don't know.

DOBBS All the old lies, the old accusations? Everything wrong in his life is Joe Dobbs? Well, look at him, for God's sake.

MALLEY How can you hate me so much . . . How can so much hate exist?

REESE What calls is he talking about, what pictures?

DOBBS I don't know!

MALLEY *You're lying!*

REESE Joe, what were you doing to him?

DOBBS Nothing!

MALLEY Destroying me! With all, *all* the malevolence in him! (*He springs up and rushes at* DOBBS, *hands raised*) Devil! (DOBBS *moves back quickly.* REESE *is too stunned to move immediately*) Devil! (*Now* REESE *comes behind him and grabs him just as he is about to strike* DOBBS) DEVIL!

REESE Jerome, no!

MALLEY (*Trying to break away*) Wasn't it enough— me? Me? (*He frees himself and turns to face* REESE) And he's got you all, hasn't he? Every last one of you. (*He begins to move out of the room*) Well, I'll show you, I'll find a way to show you the evil he's brought down on every last one of you. (*He is mounting the stairs. Stops*) But I'll bring you down with me . . . Mr. Dobbs!

    (*He disappears up the stairs.* REESE *moves toward the door suddenly.* DOBBS *steps into the doorway*)

REESE (*Calls*) Jerome!

DOBBS   Let him go!

REESE   Get out of my way, Joe!

DOBBS   I said let him go!

REESE (*Pushing* DOBBS *aside*)   I've got to help him!

(REESE *is rushing up the stairs*)

DOBBS (*Steps into the hall*)   Did you hear me?

REESE   He can't go up like that! Jerome!

(REESE *disappears upstairs*)

DOBBS (*Enormous power*)   LET HIM GO! (*There is a sudden great sound—a shriek of boys' voices. The shriek fills the room, the school. Another sound—a rush, the toppling of furniture.* DOBBS *stands rooted by the terrible sounds.* FATHER GRIFFIN *rushes down the stairs*) What is it? What's happened?

FATHER GRIFFIN   My God! Jerome! He's—jumped, he—! Keep those kids up here, we've got to keep them out of the courtyard!

(*He runs down the stairs. The boys appear at the top of the staircase, screaming. They come down*

to the landing and stop when they see DOBBS.
Silence)

DOBBS (*As the boys rush down*)   All right, you boys,
listen to me . . . stay here . . .

(*One of the boys moves slowly toward* DOBBS, *his
face lighting up with some kind of terrible recognition.* DOBBS *puts out his hands to stop the boy. The
boy pulls back violently. His hands rise suddenly
and come down with a cry against* DOBBS' *face.*
DOBBS *staggers under the blow, and falls to his knees
as* REESE *comes down the stairs. The boys surround*
DOBBS *now, striking him; he is trying to protect
himself.* REESE *fights his way to him, pulling the
boys off. The boys continue down the stairs.* REESE
is standing over DOBBS *now, looking down at him.*
DOBBS *looks up, a plea for help.* REESE *turns away
and goes downstairs.* DOBBS *is alone, a single spot on
him now. He pulls himself up slowly and moves
toward the Faculty Room. The sounds in the building diminish gradually.* DOBBS *falls into a chair,
staring at nothing. Long wait. Silence. The light
builds slowly.* DOBBS *has not moved. Three boys
appear, on the upper landing, from the gym area,
and on the staircase from the lower floor. They are
moving toward the statue. A door slams downstairs.
The boys stand still and wait.* REESE *comes up the
stairs. He stops when he sees the boys. They exchange a long look of recognition.* REESE *moves
past them, to the Faculty Room. The boys assume*

*set positions in the corridor, their eyes on the
Faculty Room as* REESE *opens the door and enters)*

REESE (*Pause; at door*) Maybe you haven't heard, old
man: this building is closed. They want us out of here.
What are you waiting for? There's nothing left.

DOBBS (*Without looking up*) I've been sitting here,
thinking . . . Those boys . . . couldn't have known what
they were doing. To hit me? I mean, what reason would
any of my boys have to do something like that to the
old man?

REESE What old man are you talking about? The one I
saw beaten to his knees an hour ago?

DOBBS You need a longer memory than that, boy.

REESE (*A step into the room*) I've got one, Joe. I remember all the beers and the handouts. Well, a quick
beer isn't going to help me forget what happened here
today. Jerome is dead.

DOBBS (*Looks up*) Well, then God rest his soul.

REESE And that's all you've got to say?

DOBBS What do you want, boy—tears? (*Another boy*

comes up the stairs and stops on the second step from the top) Well, I have no tears for Jerome.

REESE   Then maybe I have enough for both of us. I could have stopped him. But you wouldn't let me go up there. Why?

DOBBS   Why should you stop him? What did Jerome ever do for you boys? That door was always open to you boys whenever you needed me. Any of you felt free to come in and talk to me until he moved in here . . . *(A boy appears on the balcony in the Faculty Room.* DOBBS *does not see him)* All right, it's back the way it should be, so what does it matter that Jerome is dead?

REESE   My God! What are you?

DOBBS   What I've always been to all you boys. And you know it. That's why I say those boys didn't know what they were doing.

REESE   And did they know what they were doing to themselves downstairs after they sent you crawling back into this room? You want to know what your boys were doing to each other?

DOBBS   No . . .

REESE   Kids fighting for bits of broken glass . . . to tear themselves . . . (*Another boy appears at the opposite end of the balcony*) your boys, all of them your boys . . .

DOBBS   Is that why you've come back? To blame me for what's happened to my school, my boys?

REESE   You don't need me for that, Joe. Your boys showed you that out in the hall.

DOBBS   I told you . . . they didn't know what they were doing.

REESE   They knew what they were doing. And everything he said was true. What were you doing to him? (*No reply.* DOBBS *is still deep within himself.* REESE *has come to the table; he sits beside* DOBBS) You wanted him dead, didn't you, Joe?

DOBBS   No. I wanted him out of my school.

REESE   Your school! What makes it *your* school?

DOBBS   Thirty years.

REESE   Thirty years of what?

DOBBS   Thirty years of my life. My life is this school. That makes it mine.

REESE Well, it's all yours now. (*Another boy appears on the stairs*) My God, you did want him dead.

DOBBS No! I never wanted that.

REESE (*Building*) You wanted him dead.

DOBBS (*Same*) I wanted him out of my life!

REESE You wanted him dead!

DOBBS (*Bursting out*) *All right, I wanted him dead!* If that's what you want me to say, then I wanted him dead! If that was the only way to get him out of my school, out of my life, then I wanted him dead!

REESE Well, he's dead. It took you ten years, didn't it, but you finally found a way to break him. Well, what are you going to do with all the hate that's in you now?

DOBBS There's no more hate left in me.

REESE Of course not. (*A boy moves down a step*) You've managed to infect this whole place with it . . . this room is *filled* with it . . . And, Joe, you've infected your boys, every last one of them. (*Looks at his hand*) Is that what I tried to tear out of myself. The hate?

DOBBS My boys? I've never done anything to hurt my boys.

(*A boy enters the corridor from the gym. He moves down opposite the Faculty Room door and leans against the rail*)

REESE You still think you're the grand old man of the faculty. Well, you're not, Joe. You're a killer. (*The boys are moving toward the door: one step*) And Jerome was only one victim. (REESE *opens the Faculty Room door, and a boy throws open the locker-room door. He is in the room*) The others are here. They're still your boys. They've come back for the old man. Maybe they'll forgive you for what you've done.

DOBBS My boys . . . ?

REESE Are you afraid, Joe?

DOBBS I've never been afraid of any of my boys.

(DOBBS *starts to get up*)

REESE Well then, I'll leave you with them. After all, what's the old man without his boys?

(REESE *leaves the room. He stops in the corridor, and looks at the boys waiting. Then he moves past them and down the stairs. The boys enter the room slowly.* DOBBS *moves to the center of the room*)

DOBBS (*Calling as he moves back*) Paul? Paul, wait? (*The boys are circling him. He does not move as he looks at each of them*) McArdle? Jennings? Carre? Medley? Shea? Wilson? Banks? Travis? (*A pause. They are very close to him. He raises his hands, just slightly*) Please. (*Quietly*) Please?

(*They close in on him*)

Curtain

About the Author

ROBERT MARASCO is thirty-three, a native New Yorker. After graduation from college, he worked as an office boy at *The New Yorker*. He decided to try teaching for a year, but ended up staying for nine years at a Catholic prep school as an instructor of Latin, Greek and English. The experience, he insists, was pleasant.

Child's Play is Mr. Marasco's first Broadway play. He has recently completed a screenplay, *Burnt Offerings*.